HITLER
IN CARTOONS

HITLER IN CARTOONS

Lampooning the Evil Madness of a Dictator

Edited by
Tony Husband

ARCTURUS

This edition published in 2016 by Arcturus Publishing Limited
26/27 Bickels Yard, 151–153 Bermondsey Street,
London SE1 3HA

ISBN: 978-1-78599-355-8
AD004917US

Printed in China

Contents

INTRODUCTION

At the beginning of the 1920s, everyone seemed to underestimate Adolf Hitler. After all, no one could have foreseen the full horror of what he was about to inflict on the world. But when this awkward figure of a man stepped on stage and started ranting about the *Vaterland*, vast numbers of people proved only too willing to listen to what he was saying.

He became the Germans' dark Messiah, the sick-minded visionary at the heart of the nation, driving it on to increasingly reckless acts of folly. Soon the Nazis were marching across Europe, committing unspeakable crimes in the name of the Third Reich.

Perhaps because he was a gift to draw, with his cow's lick hairstyle and pencil mustache, cartoonists latched on to Hitler quickly—much more quickly than the majority of politicians.

By the late 1930s, a significant number of European leaders were in favor of appeasing the Nazis. Some of them claimed Hitler had brought order and prosperity back to his country; but it is more likely that

they were too afraid of Germany's growing military might to voice any oppostion to their dangerous neighbor.

Cartoonists are a skeptical lot. They're trained to look behind false rhetoric and seek out the inner person—to home in on weaknesses and frailties—and then, with a joke and a few skilful brushstrokes, reveal the truth behind the headlines.

At first, many cartoon images of Hitler and his acolytes were simply mocking, but the nature of the drawings darkened as the horrific reality of his regime emerged.

German cartoonists who had been depicting Hitler as deluded, depraved, or dim were doing a decent job of showing him up for what he was, but they fell silent as the power of the Nazis grew.

The reason was simple. After Hitler seized power in 1933, any publication that opposed him was shut down or co-opted to the Nazi cause. Many artists and writers were either imprisoned or forced into exile.

Some sought refuge in neighboring countries, only to have to flee for their lives

"An Early Gathering of the Nazi Party in Germany" by Tony Husband (2016): Adolf Hitler and his Nazi henchmen attempt to hold a rally in the center of some unnamed German city, but passers-by pay them little heed since they are too busy looking to see what on earth they're pointing at.

THE GREAT DECLINE.

TUESDAY, MARCH 23, 1943.

as triumphant German forces crossed more and more borders, exporting Nazi dogma and intolerance as they did so.

Domestically, repression worsened as Germany's misfortunes grew, particularly in the wake of Stalingrad, and jokes against the regime were no longer tolerated.

In 1943, when someone snitched on Berlin munitions worker Marianne Elise Kürchner for telling a joke about Hitler and Hermann Goering, she was guillotined for "undermining the war

ABOVE: "The Great Decline" by Daniel R. Fitzpatrick, 1943: Hitler discovers that he too is going up in smoke along with Stalingrad. Two-time Pulitzer Prize-winner Daniel Fitzpatrick, who worked for the *St.Louis Post-Despatch*, was a great champion of democracy. His first anti-Nazi cartoons appeared in the 1930s and he did as much as anybody to turn American public opinion against Hitler.

RIGHT: Fake stamp ("Busted Reich") printed by the Office of Strategic Services, forerunner of the CIA, and placed on propaganda letters dropped into Germany in 1941 in the hope they would slip unnoticed into the German postal system.

OPPOSITE: Walter Trier's marvelous portrait (c. 1942) of the Nazi family and the high and low culture that inspired them, featuring Streicher, Hess, Himmler, Goering, and Goebbels among others. Trier was a German-speaking Jew from Prague who produced leaflets for the Ministry of Information, London after fleeing Germany in 1936. He famously illustrated *Emil and the Detectives*.

effort," even though Hitler was well-known for telling jokes about members of his entourage, especially Goering (though not about himself!).

Similarly, it was not advisable to call one of your pets "Adolf," as there were special courts available to try you if you did, and Nazi judges were not renowned for their sense of humor. Dictators and their hangers-on function best in a climate of fear. Humor is their Achilles heel, so anyone who mocks them does so at their peril.

Hitler's power depended on the idea that he was invincible, which is why he and his propagandists created the myth of a perfect being called the *Führer*, whose judgement could never be questioned. This was like a red rag to a bull for cartoonists, who mocked Hitler's grandiosity with visual depictions of a puffed-up, deluded tyrant.

At the same time, many Germans became true believers. They swallowed Nazi propaganda undiluted and the scales didn't fall from their eyes until Hitler and Eva Braun

committed suicide in their Berlin bunker and the Red Flag was flying over the ruins of the Reichstag (the German parliament) in 1945.

It can be hard to understand how Hitler got away with it. Today, world leaders are under constant scrutiny on Facebook, Twitter, and other networking systems—every stammer, twitch, and nuance is noted—but last century tyrants could literally get away with murder because the media had far fewer outlets and these could be controlled relatively easily. Hitler had ample opportunity to build up his *Führer* mystique.

But nothing eludes the gaze of cartoonists. They saw the madness in his eyes and they started ringing the alarm bells.

You can see great examples of what they came up with in these pages: Hitler's mouth as the barrel of a gun, talking peace, but built to spit out death; or Hitler actually in league with Death. Yet another image from 1933 shows him carrying a torch burning with racial hatred. Across the world, cartoonists lined up to hit Hitler where it hurt. And somehow it's still satisfying to imagine him jumping up and down with rage at their drawings. To get them back, Hitler drew up a blacklist of cartoonists—names of those to be "dealt with" when victory came.

In my mind's eye, I picture Hitler conquering the world and immediately opening up a special prison for cartoonists.

MORE WISHFUL THINKING

"Can Spring be far behind?"
"I don't know, but the Russians aren't."

"More Wishful Thinking" by Illingworth (1942): Joseph Goebbels and Adolf Hitler attempt to warm themselves at a brazier on the Eastern Front. As the cold weather begins to bite, they start questioning the wisdom of invading Russia.

OPPOSITE: "The Old Fourth of July with New Significance" by Jay "Ding" Darling (1943): Members of Murder Incorporated (Hitler, Mussolini and Tojo) find themselves flying through the air on the firecracker of freedom, which is about to explode somewhere deep in space. Darling is reminding us of the purpose of U.S. war efforts.

© 1999 J.N. "Ding" Darling Foundation

A book called *Hitler in Cartoons of the World—Facts versus Ink* appeared in 1933. It featured a cartoon about Hitler on the left-hand page of each spread, with a Nazi rant on the other, rebutting the message of the drawing. But words can't beat pictures, so it all fell a bit flat. It was still a best-seller, though. Later Hanfstaengl fell out badly with Hitler and headed for the U.S. with his ill-gotten gains.

Still, it's safe to conclude there was nothing Hitler hated more than being made a laughing stock by cartoonists. He had good reason. All the jokes about him and the Nazis—day after day in

He might have had them mounted on plaques like Big Game trophies, pens in hand and with ink as their blood, but somehow, I think, they'd still have found a way of making him look a fool.

Like many famous people, Hitler collected cartoons about himself. In a vain attempt to protect his image, he employed press officers to go through the world's newspapers and bring offending items to his attention. One day his Harvard-educated Press Secretary Ernst "Titch" Hanfstaengl came up with an idea that was to make him a fortune.

paper after paper, like an endlessly dripping tap—built up until they played a big part in shaping U.S. public opinion, for example in persuading Americans to come in on the side of the Allies.

A legion of top cartoonists had toiled away ceaselessly until their image of Hitler was the one the world came to accept (and still does), and for that we should be truly grateful. Without their efforts, we might not enjoy the freedoms of today.

Tony Husband

Hitler's first major speech in the Reichstag, the German parliament, in 1933 was a plea for peace, equal rights and mutual understanding between nations. Some gullible people actually believed he meant what he said, but not Georges in *The Nation*, New York, 1933, who produced the powerful image above.

Chapter 1

On the Way UP

The central idea behind much German propaganda of the 1930s and 1940s was that Hitler was a godlike genius, who would lead the Master Race to a German Reich which would last a thousand years. Shaped by grievance at the Treaty of Versailles and tempered by Nazi terror, it was a collective national fantasy that came to grief against overwhelming odds in 1945 as Germany was invaded from all sides. In the early years, however, Hitler enjoyed a remarkable winning streak which carried him ever upward in the Nazi Party, and then to the summit of the German state. But who would finally win the battle for minds? The Nazis were masters of propaganda, but they were powerless against a well-timed joke.

"Hitler the Saviour" by George Grosz (1923): This drawing mocks a popular postcard of the time by photographer Heinrich Hoffmann, which featured Hitler in a trenchcoat. Alluding to the Grimms' fairytale about a man in a bearskin who made a pact with the devil as well as Wagner's *Ring Cycle*, Grosz concludes that Hitler is a throwback to another age. This portrait was included in the Nazis' Degenerate Art Exhibition, 1937.

"Consolation" by Thomas Theodor Heine (1924): Hitler left Landsberg Prison in 1924, having written *Mein Kampf* while serving a prison sentence for his part in the Munich Putsch. Here, he is being handed his uniform by fellow fascist Hermann Kriebel who is saying: "Don't worry about it, Adolf. In Germany making a fool of yourself isn't fatal. If it didn't work out for you as a sergeant, let's try again as Reichspräsident."

Ergebnislose Haussuchung bei Hitler

(Th. Th. Heine)

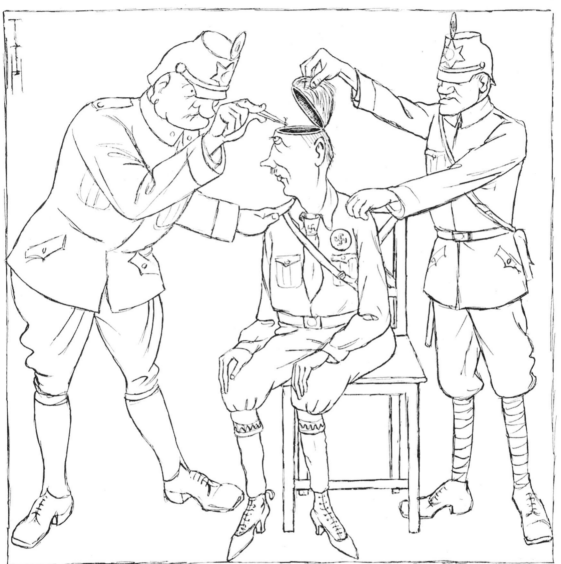

„Merkwürdig, mit wie geringen Mitteln sich viel Unheil anrichten läßt!"

"Inconclusive Search at Hitler's Place" by Thomas Theodor Heine (1930): As
the economic crisis grew in Germany, the number of police searches of people's
homes increased. At the same time, the Nazis were seeking to become electable
and even had Hitler kissing babies. Here, the police aren't finding much. One says:
"Remarkable how so much disaster has sprung from so small a seed." Cartoonist
Thomas Theodor Heine fled to Prague in 1933 when the Nazis came to power.

An die deutschen Mussolinischwärmer
Die um Hitler

„Du haft mich beraubt,   Und angespuckt,
Du haft mich gebuckt,   Sogar mißhandelt haft du mich:
Du haft mich beleidigt   Trotz alledem — bewundere ich dich!"

An image probably from the 1920s which is sarcastically dedicated to the German fans of Mussolini and Hitler: Hitler remains obedient to the overbearing Italian: "You've robbed me, insulted me, beaten me up and spat on me. Despite all the bullying, I worship you." At this stage, Mussolini was still the model for Hitler, who tried to emulate his March on Rome with the Munich Putsch, but Hitler's admiration was later to turn to scorn.

"Responsibility" (1931): This appeared in Social Democratic satire magazine *Der Wahre Jacob* in 1931. It says: "Responsibility is getting nearer and the closer it gets, the longer Adolf's face becomes," suggesting Hitler wasn't up to the job of running Germany. The magazine was closed down by the Nazis in 1933.

Die Verantwortung rückt näher und nähe
Je kürzer die Frist ist, desto länger wir
Adolfs Gesicht.

"Only the stupidest cows vote for their own butcher" by Rudolf Herrmann (1932): This image was chosen for the front cover of *Roter Pfeffer* (Red Pepper) magazine with the aim of averting the calamity of Hitler being elected. In 1932 there were 6 million unemployed in Germany and the NSDAP (the Nazis) won 37.4 percent of the vote in the July elections; the Nazis were inching closer to power on a diet of discontent.

"The Führer's Lament – 'How can I become a dictator if no one helps me?'" (1932): This appeared in *Der Wahre Jaccob* in 1932 as well as Ernst Hanfstaengl's book of cartoons in 1933—see page 11. The book sought to take the sting out of anti–Hitler cartoons, in this case by claiming that Hitler's triumphs since taking power already answered the question. "Either Hitler's successes belong to him alone, or he had help. If the first is true, he needs no help; and if the second is true, he had help." But Hanfstaengl was wasting his time trying to outdo this image!

In this stylish cartoon by British artist Thomas Derrick from *The Bookman* magazine in 1933, Hitler abandons the ark carrying League of Nations diplomats during a deluge and makes off on his own in a canoe. Hitler had ordered his delegates to quit disarmament talks in Geneva and pulled Germany out of the League of Nations, forerunner of the U.N. Hitler claimed Germany had disarmed, but that other nations weren't following suit.

ABOVE: "Hitler and Krupp—His Master's Voice" (1933): This fine drawing appeared in Brussels paper *Le Soir*. It features Adolf Hitler as a dog with swastika markings about to fire arms manufacturer Gustav Krupp out of his own gun. The implication is that Hitler was controlling his rich industrialist backers rather than the other way around.

OPPOSITE: "Some Dictators Don't Know Where to Stop" by Jay "Ding" Darling (1933): The racist policies of Nazi Germany sought to stimulate the "Aryan" birthrate through generous government loans, while limiting others. Jay Norwood Darling, better known as Ding Darling, worked for the *New York Herald* from 1917 to 1949 and won two Pulitzer Prizes.

De Compagnons
Die Verbündeten

"De Compagnons" (1933): Hitler and his companion Death stalk the
land, leaving behind a trail of victims as they plot their next move. In
January 1933, Hitler became Chancellor of Germany, and the Nazis
continued to unleash wave after wave of extreme violence upon their
opponents. In March 1933, the first official government concentration
camp was established at Dachau. It was to be the template for all others.

"Pyromaniac" by Rollin Kirby (1933): Carrying the torches of race hatred and repression, Hitler strides through Germany. This is an image that evokes the torchlit processions celebrating Hitler's coming to power. At this time, sections of the press in the U.S. were still pro-Hitler. People believed that Hitler would water down his demands in office, a view very much shared in Washington. This cartoon argues the opposite.

"The Vote" by Paule Loring (1933): The year 1933 marked the last multi-party vote before World War II. The Nazis' violently anti-semitic, anti-communist electoral campaign was orchestrated by Joseph Goebbels, while Hermann Goering ordered SS and SA thugs to "monitor" the election—meaning they intimidated voters using violence. Following the campaign of terror, the Nazi vote increased to 43.9 percent, and Germany was transformed by brutal and nefarious means from a democracy to a dictatorship in double-quick time.

THE BEST-SELLER.

[1,000,000 copies of HERR HITLER's Life-story have already been published in Germany.]

"The Best-Seller" by Leonard Raven-Hill (1933): In this drawing from *Punch* magazine, a familiar face performs the hard-sell on his own political autobiography, *Mein Kampf* ["My Struggle"]. This cartoon mocks both the dubious quality of the book, and the manner in which Hitler gained power. When Hitler ran Germany, a copy of *Mein Kampf* was handed out free to every newly married couple, and to every soldier fighting at the front. By 1945, 10 million copies had been distributed, but how many people actually read it?

"The Misfit" by Edwin Marcus (1933): As The World watches from the brow of a hill, an undersized Hitler—instantly recognizable by his mustache—tries on the trappings of leadership for size and is found wanting; he's wearing the old Kaiser Bill uniform with huge black boots, enormous sword (labeled "Dictatorship"), and a helmet which has slipped down over his eyes. The imperial eagle waves a swastika to indicate the change of regime. In 1933, Hitler was thought by many outside Germany to be just the "window dressing" for the Nazis, and that Hermann Goering was the real power behind the throne.

By permission of the Marcus family

"Hanging on to the Demagogue" by Rollin Kirby (1933): A respectable German citizen tries to keep Hitler in check as he emerges from a landscape of jingoism, reaction, and race hatred bearing a flag with a swastika on it. Hindenburg had appointed Hitler chancellor in a coalition government, but so far there were no indications that he was going to be moderating his political demands. Quite the contrary!

Stylized cartoon from French newspaper *L'Intransigeant* (1933) with Hitler as Nero after right-wing German students had publicly burned bonfires of books across Germany. The roll of honor of authors whose work was destroyed included Gide, Marx, Thomas Mann, Proust, Zola, H. G. Wells, Jack London, Brecht, Einstein, and Erich Maria Remarque. Nineteenth-century German writer Heinrich Heine once prophesied with uncanny accuracy: "Where they start burning books, they end up burning people too."

"Warning to the French! Hitler Is Demolishing Peace" from the Propaganda Center of the French Republicans (1933): Like Samson in the temple of the Philistines, Hitler knocks over the pillars, heedless of the damage he could be doing himself and to those around him. After Hitler withdrew from the League of Nations talks in 1933, he complained that the Treaty of Versailles had left Germany at too great a disadvantage for peace to last, but in reality peace was the last thing on his mind.

"The Eternal Drummer" by Olaf Gulbransson (1933): Before the Munich People's Court in 1924, Hitler defined his aim within the Party: "It was not out of modesty that I wanted to become a drummer. It's the crucial role…" Here, Joseph Goebbels is saying: "Roll up, roll up, Ladies and Gentlemen, for the very last time the Third Reich is about to begin. [*in Hitler's ear*] Man, if we don't get going soon, the crowd will have gone."

Will Dyson, *Daily Herald*, 1934, the British Cartoon Archive, University of Kent, www.cartoons.ac.uk

"Storm Troopers" by Will Dyson (1934): Dyson shows a two-faced Hitler after the "Night of the Long Knives," actually three days during which 150–200 of Hitler's "own kind" were killed. When the SA [the vicious paramilitary wing of the Nazi Party] threatened to become too powerful—it had more than two million members—Hitler came to an agreement with the German army that he would have its leading members shot, including Ernst Röhm.

"And the *Führer* said, 'Only death can drive us apart.'" (1934): Swiss cartoon
showing Hitler standing like an ex-lover by the freshly dug graves of SA leader
Ernst Röhm and his deputy Edmund Heines. Top Nazis sought status through
Hitler and jealousies were rife. Accordingly, lies were fed by Himmler and Heydrich
to Hitler suggesting that the powerful Röhm was planning a coup. Röhm was arrested
and given a gun with a single bullet with which to end his life. He wouldn't, or couldn't,
do the deed, and the psychotic Theodor Eicke, Kommandant of Dachau, stepped up to
pull the trigger. Röhm's dying words were almost touching: "*Führer, mein Führer.*" This
deadly business meant Hitler now enjoyed total control over Germany.

"Hitler the Butcher of Berlin" by Ralph Soupault (1934): A blood-spattered Hitler stands over the corpses of his victims after settling scores during the Night of the Long Knives. The cartoonist Ralph Soupault was an extreme French nationalist who later joined the PPF, the French fascist party. For supporting the occupying German forces in France during the war years, he was sentenced to 15 years in jail in 1946.

"Drifting with the Whitsuntide" by Will Dyson (1934): Snoring gently, the world drifts out to sea during a British public holiday while Hitler, Prime Minister Ramsay MacDonald, Mussolini, Hirohito, and Foreign Secretary John Simon debate the merits of disarmament with no great success. The Germans had already repudiated the League of Nations, and the Japanese really were no better, having invaded Manchuria in 1931.

Will Dyson, *Daily Herald*, 1934, the British Cartoon Archive, University of Kent, www.cartoons.ac.uk

A GOOD BOY FOR ONCE.

Der Führer. "Fancy! This is the first row I haven't been in for years."

"A Good Boy For Once" by E. H. Shepard (1935): While the rest of the world squabbles over plans for peace, Hitler gives the impression that butter wouldn't melt in his mouth. Germany was busy in 1935, including making the announcement that the nation was to re-arm in violation of the Treaty of Versailles—quickly followed by an order for a dozen submarines. The Nuremberg Laws robbing Jews of rights were also imposed.

"Guignol de Nuremberg" by Edouard Halouze (1936): Guignol was the main character in a French puppet show who took many roles. Here, he takes the shape of Hitler, who is about to bash Stalin with his truncheon. They're in a play called *Reach for the Stars*—words by Adolf Hitler and music by Richard Wagner. But this is really about the anti-Comintern pact between Nazi Germany and Japan designed to put the squeeze on the Soviet Union.

An illustration which shows Hitler and his men watching black U.S. sprinter Jesse Owens during the 1936 Olympics in Berlin by U.S. illustrator and Olympic fencer Ed Vebell. With immense cunning, Germany camouflaged its racist and anti-democratic agenda for the duration of the Games and ended up winning the most medals of any country after the democracies had vetoed the idea of a boycott. Vebell was a regular contributor to *Reader's Digest*. He also worked for *Stars and Stripes*, the U.S. military newspaper, during World War II, and was an official court artist at the Nuremberg Trials.

"Almeria Incident" by Willard Combes (1937): After an air raid by Soviet bombers on the port of Ibiza in the Mediterranean in which the German heavy cruiser *Deutschland* was badly damaged and crew members killed, German naval forces responded by shelling Almeria, causing widespread panic and killing at least 19 people, with 55 seriously wounded.

OPPOSITE: "Hitler Speaking" by Victor Weisz (1937): Born in Berlin to Hungarian-Jewish parents, "Vicky," as he was known, worked for an anti-Nazi journal called *12 Uhr Blatt*, which was taken over by the Nazis in 1933, forcing Weisz to move to London in 1935. Vicky wanted his cartoons to "engineer opinion." For subjects he felt most strongly about, he developed an expressionist style with heavy shadows reminiscent of artist Käthe Kollwitz.

On the Way Up

"The Goat and the Swines" by Marti Bofarull (1937): This is about the Spanish Civil War. The Non-Intervention Committee is pictured as a two-headed goat, with the faces of French Prime Minister Leon Blum and British Prime Minister Stanley Baldwin, suckling Hitler and Mussolini. In September 1936 under pressure from Britain and France, a Non-Intervention Agreement was signed by 27 countries, including Germany, Italy, the Soviet Union, and Italy. Despite this, Italy and Germany continued to help Franco.

"And Now Hitler is Going to 'Purge' German Art" by Herb Block (1937): The *Haus der Deutschen Kunst*, Munich opened in 1937. This Nazi art gallery featured only "approved art"—for example, peasant idylls, idealized portraits of German workers and families, neoclassical nudes in pseudo-Hellenic settings, and heroic military missions expressing love and longing for the Fatherland. Art was only encouraged if it served Nazi doctrine.

YET ONE MORE CONVERSATION

" *The time had come,*" *Herr* HITLER *said,*
" *To talk of many things,*
Of might and right and swastikas
And triangles and rings,

And why the world is boiling hot,
And whether Peace has wings."
Lord HALIFAX. "*But not about Colonies.*"
Herr HITLER. "*Hush!*"

"Yet One More Conversation" by Bernard Partridge (1937): Referencing Lewis Carroll's *Alice Through the Looking Glass*, Hitler plays the Walrus to Lord Halifax's Carpenter. Prime Minister Neville Chamberlain sent Foreign Secretary Lord Halifax, his fellow appeaser, to talk once again to Hitler, Goebbels, and Goering in 1937. When Winston Churchill became PM in 1940, Halifax was instantly exiled to the British Embassy in Washington.

"But We Don't Want War" by Will Dyson (c.1937). Such august personages as Mussolini, Ernest Bevin, Hirohito, and Neville Chamberlain hug the chimney stacks of the arms industry for warmth as the world heads toward inevitable conflagration. Adolf Hitler is holding a mini version of Lloyd George in the palm of his hand because the Welsh politician had represented Britain during negotiations over the Treaty of Versailles, arguing the case for Germany to retain some of its arms as a bulwark against the spread of the Russian Revolution.

Will Dyson, *Daily Herald*, c.1937, the British Cartoon Archive, University of Kent, www.cartoons.ac.uk

"Hygiene of the Race" by Albin Amelin (c.1939): This dark image comes from Swedish artist Albin Amelin, a communist who "worked in rich colours and rough contours." By the outbreak of World War II, organized slaughter by the Nazis was already in full flow. First it was people with mental and physical disabilities considered by the Nazis to be a burden on the state and a threat to Germany's "racial hygiene." Quickly they were followed by the Jews and other minorities.

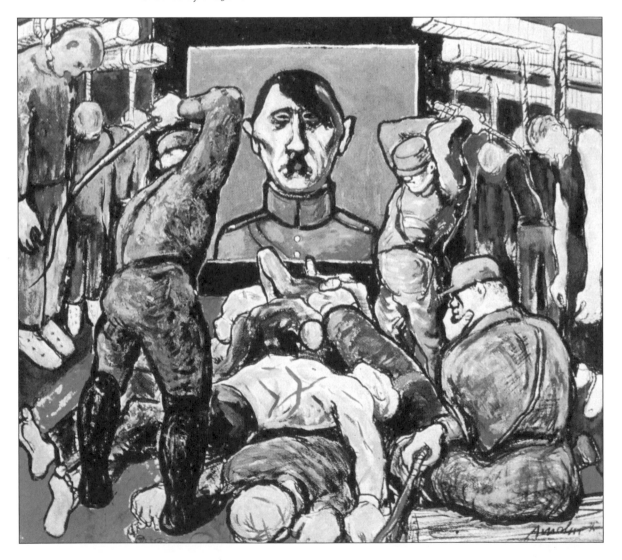

"The Rev. Martin Niemoeller, A.D. 1938" by D. R. Fitzpatrick (1938): Niemoeller was a conservative Protestant pastor, who had initially welcomed Hitler to power. He was interned in Sachsenhausen (and later Dachau) concentration camps for objecting to the Nazi takeover of the Protestant church organizations. It was he who said: "First they came for the Socialists, and I did not speak out—Because I was not a Socialist. Then they came for the Trade Unionists, and I did not speak out—Because I was not a Trade Unionist. Then they came for the Jews, and I did not speak out—Because I was not a Jew. Then they came for me—and there was no one left to speak for me."

INCREASING PRESSURE.

ABOVE: "Increasing Pressure" by David Low (1938): In 1938, Germany took over Austria after *Anschluss* [annexation], and this cartoon suggests that the widespread policy of appeasement was only leading to Germany throwing its weight around throughout Europe.

RIGHT: "'My Benito!' 'My Adolf!'" by D. R. Fitzpatrick (1938): Hitler and Mussolini met up in a train carriage by the Brenner Pass in 1938 to pledge friendship. But past disputes were not forgotten, according to Fitzpatrick.

"MY BENITO!" "MY ADOLF!"

Will Dyson, *Daily Herald*, c.1937, the British Cartoon Archive, University of Kent, www.cartoons.ac.uk

"Abyss of Reaction" by Will Dyson (undated, but probably c.1937): Hitler was a huge admirer of Bismarck, the reactionary Prussian politician who brought about the unification of Germany in 1871; this new entity immediately began to menace the rest of Europe. In his usual muscular style, Dyson is reminding us that Hitler followed in a long line of blinkered, militaristic tyrants, but that he might be worse than all the others combined.

THE DAWN OF A DOUBT

Master Adolf. "It tasted lovely—but I'm beginning to wonder whether it's not going to disagree with me!"

"The Dawn of a Doubt" by Bernard Partridge (1938): In 1938, Germany annexed Austria, swallowing it whole. This cartoon suggests that this was an act which could rebound on the Fatherland. Interestingly, Hitler didn't much care for exercise, but he had a sweet tooth. When he stayed at his retreat, the Berghof, he used to walk down to the village shop to buy lots of cream cakes, then get his chauffeur to ferry him back up the hill to eat them.

NEIGHBOURLY CONDUCT

Herr Hitler. "Extraordinary how the least little bit of noise seems to upset some parties."

"Neighbourly Conduct" by Bernard Partridge (1938): France and Britain peer over the garden fence to see where all the noise is coming from as Adolf Hitler reinforces his stockade. Turning a blind eye to German intentions was becoming impossible. It wasn't as if the Nazis were operating by stealth either. The drumbeats were getting louder and louder as Germany contemplated annexing the Sudetenland as the prelude to further misdeeds.

TOYS AND THE MAN

"All meant for you, lady."

[Herr HITLER in his address to the heads of the Diplomatic Corps at Berlin laid stress on Germany's desire for peace.]

Opposite: "Toys and the Man" by E. H. Shepard (1938): With a nod to Hitler's semi-vagrant past, Shepard has Hitler on the street selling toy soldiers which he is trying to pass off as suitable offerings for the Angel of Peace. *Arms and the Man* (1894) was a play by George Bernard Shaw about the futility of war.

PURGE, OR THE BERLIN CHARIVARI

Above: "Purge, or the Berlin Charivari" by E. H. Shepard (1938): Hitler sacked War Minister Werner von Blomberg for marrying a convicted prostitute and Commander-in-Chief Werner von Fritsch, allegedly for being a homosexual. Pressing home his advantage, he replaced other senior officers in the army with men sympathetic to the Nazi cause. Result? The regular army came into line, and Goebbels who planned it all enhanced his standing.

"The New Pilgrim of Peace" (c.1940): Concealing the brutally slain corpse of Poland behind his back, Hitler waves his olive branch in the direction of Britain and France. By this time, nobody was in any doubt about the intentions of the *Führer*.

Chapter 2

Jackboots on the
MARCH

What effect do cartoons have in the real world where power is backed up by force of arms? Napoleon famously said that British cartoonist James Gillray, who attacked him again and again, did more to damage his campaigns than a dozen generals ever could have. King Louis-Philippe of France had cartoonist Honoré Daumier put in jail, claiming "a caricature amounts to an act of violence." When Hitler's armies started to march across Europe, cartoonists were called up by the democracies to mobilize public opinion. They produced highly effective propaganda. In the case of Hitler, cartoonists were drawing evil incarnate and, during World War II, it became their patriotic duty to paint his portrait with a poison pen.

"One At A Time Please" by Jay "Ding" Darling, (1939): Britain suffered an *annus horribilis* in 1939. The Japanese army blockaded British settlements in China and there were anti-British riots in Tokyo; Russia broke her pact with Britain and France, then sided with bullying Germany, which invaded Poland, taking Britain to war. Dealing with all this was ineffectual prime minister, Neville Chamberlain, whose only means of defence was a furled umbrella.

— Viens, mon pote... ton heure est arrivée...

Dessin de ELSEN.

"Come On, Old Chum… Your Time Is Up." (c.1940): A brutal, beefed-up, sweating Hitler takes a cow that has been branded with swastikas, and which probably represents France but could be Poland, off for slaughter. Artist Theodore van Elsen was a Paris printmaker and painter.

© 1999 J.N. "Ding" Da...

"Waiting For The Sword to Fall" by Jay "Ding" Darling (1939): The notion that Hitler was destroying all that was good in Europe began to catch on widely in America during the summer of 1939. Perhaps influenced by cartoons in movie theaters, Darling distorts perspective so that the sword (and thus power) wielded by the relatively small, furious figure of Hitler is immense, while European civilization (personified by a woman) is helpless and in need of rescue.

"Give Him an Inch and He Takes a Mile" by Jay "Ding" Darling (1939): Having ignored Hitler's annexation of the Sudetenland, the German-speaking part of Czechoslovakia, Britain was in a quandary over Hitler's imminent invasion of Poland. By the time this cartoon was published, Germany had concluded a non-aggression pact with the Soviet Union. The moral of this story? No one should ever have believed a single word Hitler said…

Deux têtes sous le même bonnet.

LEFT: "The Two Constrictors" by Bernard Partridge (1939): Hitler and Stalin as treacherous snakes digesting their victims—Stalin is saying: "I don't know about helping you, Adolf, but I *do* understand your point of view."

BELOW: "Adolf and the Hitchhiker" by Jay "Ding" Darling (1939): Hitler is happily pootling along in his car to the Dictators' Picnic with his pals when he stops to pick up Stalin and finds he is the victim of an armed carjack. Germany had bitten off more than it could chew when it concluded a non-aggression pact with the Soviet Union.

OPPOSITE: "Two Heads Under the Same Cap" by Henri le Monnier (1939): Stalin looks more comfortable than Hitler under the whirling joker's cap in this cartoon illustrating the French proverb meaning "hand in glove together." This was published in the French periodical *Marianne*.

"Why Ferdinand!" by Jay "Ding" Darling (1939): *The Story of Ferdinand* (1936) was a children's book by Munro Leaf about a bull that refused to fight in the bull ring. The pacifist subject matter made it a political hot potato in the 1930s. It was banned by Hitler in Germany, but Stalin allowed it to be published in Poland. Here, Musso and Hitler are taken aback at the fury inspired in the democracies by the invasion of Poland.

UN CHIEN QUI NE RAPPORTE PAS

"A Dog That Won't Fetch" by Henri le Monnier (1939): A dog with the face of Stalin carries off a hare marked "Poland and Finland." As part of the non-aggression pact with Germany, the Soviet Union had arranged to attack Poland in September 1939, but in November it demanded territory from Finland which resulted in the Winter War (1939–40), a David and Goliath affair which ended with concessions to Russia but no outright victory.

STALINE. — Un marteau ?... Voilà !

LEFT: "The Crucifixion" by Jean-Louis Chancel (1939): Hitler is trying to nail the corpse of Poland to a giant swastika when Stalin appears with the perfect tools for the job. Stalin is saying: "A hammer… I have one here!" This cartoon appeared in *Match* magazine; artist Chancel was later to become a member of the French Resistance.

RIGHT: "Just When He Was Going To Celebrate" by Edwin Marcus (1939): Most things had gone Hitler's way in 1939, but the scuttling of the battleship *Graf Spee* in Montevideo harbor after the Battle of the River Plate came as a setback. Marcus drew Hitler rather brilliantly as a pallid, middle-aged man with greasy hair and sagging skin.

By permission of the Marcus family

"Harvest Moon" by D. R. Fitzpatrick (1939): *Shine on Harvest Moon*, a Hollywood western, had been a big hit in 1938; it was directed by Joseph Kane, and starred Roy Rogers and Mary Hart. This ghostly image of Hitler as the moon hangs balefully over Planet Earth where massed ranks of artillery are drawn up in a tight circle on the battlefield. A harvest moon gives extra light, allowing farmers to keep working into the night. Fitzpatrick produced this drawing on August 25, 1939 just before the autumn equinox.

HARVEST MOON.

IT SEEMED LIKE A GOOD IDEA AT THE TIME.

"WHAT A PAL IS JOSEF!"

LEFT: Bill Mauldin defined the cartoonist's task as follows: "We are not pontificators or molders of thought… Ours is more the role of the lowly gadfly: circle and stab, circle and stab. Roughly put, our credo should be, if it's big, hit it." And that's exactly what D. R. Fitzpatrick is doing here, hitting Hitler again and again where it hurts—coming back to the subject again and again, until the character assassination is complete. "It Seemed Like A Good Idea At The Time" (1939) shows Hitler with a terrible hangover after drinking too much vodka, while "What a Pal is Josef!" (1939) emphasizes the raw deal Hitler was getting out of the mutual non-aggression pact. Both are about the same subject—Germany and the Soviet Union—and repetition hammers the message home. "Circle and stab, circle and stab!"

JOHN BULL'S WAR AIM

"John Bull"s War Aim" by Bernard Partridge (1939): The original image of a gorilla abducting a woman appeared in a sculpture by Emmanuel Frémiet in 1859. This was adopted by the Germans and the Americans during World War I for posters suggesting that Civilization was under threat and only they could save it. Here, Partridge turns Hitler into that same gorilla, six years after the first *King Kong* film was released in 1933.

NOTHING BUT DEATH CAN STOP ME NOW!

ABOVE: "Nothing But Death Can Stop Me Now!" by Clifford Berryman (1939): This cartoon appeared on September 2, 1939, the day after Germany invaded Poland. Those who had reckoned that European conflict could be averted were proved wrong and the *New York Times* commented: "The madman has unsheathed his sword, with Poland as his first victim."

OPPOSITE: "Mr Hitler Is Willing To Deal With Any Country" by Herb Block (1939): Making peace pledges was Hitler's specialty; he was always happy to make as many as you liked.

"Hotel de L'Axis" (1939): The Hotel d'Europe is under new management and it looks like they have the decorators in. Hitler reverts to his erstwhile role as house painter with Mussolini as plasterer, and they're clearly telling Uncle Sam to mind his own business. In 1939, the Roosevelt administration sent diplomatic notes to Hitler and Mussolini seeking guarantees that they wouldn't attack the other countries of Europe.

"Let All Those Who Consider War To Be the Better Solution Reject My Outstretched Hand" by Clifford Berryman (1939): In October 1939 as German and Soviet troops completed the conquest of Poland, Hitler made a speech offering peace to France and Britain. Hitler brought the speech to a climax with the words quoted here. Berryman is emphasizing the slaughter and destruction that lay behind the offer.

A French postcard of the mugging of Poland from 1940: Goering and Hitler attack from one side, while Stalin lurches into action from behind with his hammer and sickle. Hitler took a gamble by invading Poland, which perhaps failed when Britain and France came in on the side of their ally. World War II had begun.

HITLER

GOERING

LA POLOGNE

STALINE

"Germany Shall Never Be Encircled" by E. H. Shepard (1939): Hitler might desire world domination, but the task was too big for him. At a time when the Nazis were all-conquering, the cartoonist was reminding us of Hitler's limited powers.

"GERMANY SHALL NEVER BE ENCIRCLED."

"THERE'S NO REASON FOR FURTHER FIGHTING"!

POLAND

NAZI DOVE OF PEACE

ABOVE: "The Theoretician of War in his Boxer Shorts" by Ben (1939): Hitler and the German army march by in their underpants for the cover of *Le Rire* magazine as Goering says: "Oh, I'm all right. I've got my medals to protect me." Goering was notorious for his love of medals and there are very few cartoons of him where he's not wearing a great long row of them.

OPPOSITE: "Nazi Dove of Peace" by Lute Pease (1939): The Nazi dove of peace is actually a vulture preying on the fallen in Poland. .

Hitler with demonic eyes faces a U.S. soldier across the world (1939 by Herb Block): Before the United States entered the war in December 1941, public opinion had turned around from being mostly isolationist to 70 percent interventionist. Herb Block played a big role in swaying the man in the street toward intervention. He had been producing anti-isolationist cartoons on a regular basis for many years.

LEFT: "Hitler's Dream" by Paul Bachier (1939): A French propaganda postcard which shows Hitler dreaming of taking over the world and the moon, both dripping with the blood of innocents. There was no end to his madness.

RIGHT: "He'll Come Out When He's Hungry" by Philip Zec (1939): Hitler pictured as a rat by British newspaper the *Daily Mirror*.

Above are Herb Block's predictions for the year 1940, but here are some of the events which actually occurred: Dunkirk was evacuated; Hitler invaded Norway, Denmark, the Netherlands, Belgium, Luxembourg, and France as Paris fell to the Germans; Roosevelt was elected to the presidency for the third time, and the *Captain America* comic book appeared for the first time; The Battle of Britain took place in the skies over England; Winston Churchill became Prime Minister of Britain; Leon Trotsky was murdered in Mexico with an ice axe.

"Hitler Says" by Herb Block (1940): There was a sub-text to almost everything Hitler said in public, which is a fancy way of saying he lied through his teeth. In *Mein Kampf*, Hitler described The Big Lie as a key technique used by Jewish agitators—the telling of lies so colossal that no one would believe someone would have the effrontery to bend the truth so much, and would thus believe every word. Ironically, it was actually put into practice with tremendous enthusiasm by Nazi Propaganda Minister Joseph Goebbels.

LA POLITIQUE DE MONTOIRE

"The Montoire Policy" by Sennep (1940): Line drawing commemorating the famous handshake near the town of Montoire between Hitler and 84-year-old Marshal Petain signifying the start of official French collaboration during World War II. Pierre Laval had suggested the meeting which took place in a railway carriage and part of the deal with the Germans meant he now became premier. He's the one applauding in the top-right corner.

SAIREY KAMPF AND STALLY PRIG

"No, Stally! drink fair, wotever you do!"

BELOW: "What me? I never touch goldfish" by Leslie Illingworth (1940): Looking like the cats that got the cream, Hitler and Stalin bide their time as they sit purring next to the goldfish bowl waiting to launch their moves. The Axis Powers were to devastate the Balkans.

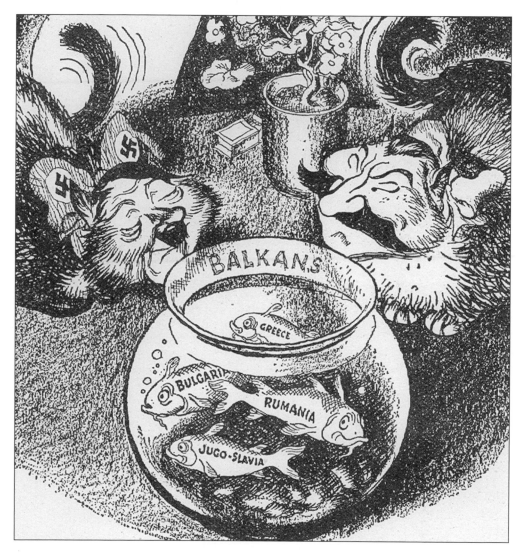

OPPOSITE: "Sairey Kampf and Stally Prig" by E. H. Shepard (1940): Inspired by two characters from Charles Dickens' *Martin Chuzzlewit*, the alcoholic midwife Sairey Gamp and her faithful companion Betsey Prig, this cartoon mocks the unequal relationship between Hitler and Stalin (where Dickens had been satirizing private nursing in Victorian times).

BELOW: Hitler is presented sympathetically in this cartoon from *Signal* magazine about the Blitzkrieg. The idea was that you couldn't guess where the Germans were going to strike next because of Hitler's brilliant and precise strategic planning. *Signal* was a glossy propaganda sheet produced by the German army and distributed abroad. At its height, its circulation was 2,5000,000. Until December 1941, you could get it in the U.S.

OPPOSITE: "Hitler's True Face!" by William Sharp (c.1940): William Sharp was an Austrian Jew (born Leon Schleifer) who produced political cartoons mocking the Nazis in the 1920s. When Hitler came to power in 1933, he was told he would be sent to a concentration camp, but managed to escape to the U.S. in 1934, moving to Forest Hills, Queens. He became a court-room artist and also worked for publications such as the *New York Times*.

Hitlers Doppelgänger

— Hallo, wer von euch Jungens hat Lust, heute Nachmittag ein Schlachtschiff einzuweihen?

FIFTH HORSEMAN OF THE APOCALYPSE.

ABOVE: Cartoon from a Swiss newspaper in the 1940s following a rumour about Hitler having several doubles. The German officer is saying: "Do any of you boys feel like launching a new battleship this afternoon?"

LEFT: "Fifth Horseman of the Apocalypse" by D. R. Fitzpatrick (1940): The German air force had played a big part in the conquest of Poland and in victories across Europe; its leader Hermann Goering became a national hero. But the Battle of Britain was about to reveal he had feet of clay.

"Falling Leaves" by Herb Block (1940): In July 1940 the blockade of Britain began. The object of the Germans was to destroy the Royal Air Force to pave the way for invasion. But during the Battle of Britain the Luftwaffe lost 1,733 aircraft to 915 RAF fighters and the Germans had to abandon their plans. Prime Minister Winston Churchill said of the RAF pilots: "Never in the history of human conflict was so much owed by so many to so few."

RIGHT: "They Call It Honour!" by Philip Zec (1940): The German authorities put pressure on neutral Sweden which had refused a request to allow German trains to transit through Sweden on their way to Narvik, the key strategic port in occupied Norway which was linked by rail to Sweden but not to Norway. Sweden soon relented and German troops passed through with impunity.

They Call It Honour!

LEFT: "Hitler Shrinking from the Ghosts of His Victims" by Harry Grissinger (c.1940): The genocidal policies of the Nazis claimed at least 11 million victims, among them communists, homosexuals, Gypsies, Slavs, Jehovah's Witnesses, Soviet POWs, Afro-Germans, the dissenting clergy, disabled people, criminals, and many more.

OPPOSITE: "Jerry-Built or The New Order" by E. H. Shepard (1940): Holding a T-square in one hand and *Mein Planpf* in the other, Hitler supervises the building of the new Europe, but it's all looking a bit rickety.

JERRY-BUILT or **THE NEW ORDER**

"Is not this great Europe which I am rebuilding?"

"Just as Napoleon Was Defeated, So Too the Conceited Hitler" by Kukryniksy (1941): Kukryniksy was the name adopted by three Russian caricaturists, Mikhail Kuprilianov, Porfirii Krylov, and Nikolai Sokolov. They produced more than 70 twisted propaganda posters for the TASS studio in Moscow during World War II.

Chapter 3

Decline and
FALL

Propaganda Minister Joseph Goebbels said that the Hitler myth was his great masterpiece, but this brilliant feat of invention rebounded on Germany when Hitler started to believe his own publicity. More and more bad decisions were made, and by the winter of 1941–2 everything began to go wrong for the Third Reich. After the cataclysmic defeat by the Russians at Stalingrad in 1943, Hitler's popularity went downhill in Germany, and not even Goebbels, who tried to repaint him as a latter-day Frederick the Great, could do much about it. But Hitler's setbacks proved to be grist to the mill of hostile cartoonists, and they celebrated his downward trajectory with greater and greater glee.

THE FATES DECIDE.

"The Fates Decide" by E. H. Shepard (1943): A brooding Hitler contemplates the coming struggle against the triumvirate of Britain, the Soviet Union, and the U.S. By 1943, it was all getting on top of him. He suffered from bowel pains, headaches, nausea, shivering fits, and diarrhea, and was visited daily by his quack Dr Theodor Morell, who gave him his regular injection and pills. He still refused to read reports containing bad news.

THE   FADING   LIGHT

"The Fading Light" by Edwin Marcus (1941): Hitler watches a sputtering candle from behind his blackout blinds. Before the Battle of Britain, the Luftwaffe had seemed invincible under Hermann Goering, but now it was apparent that it needed reinforcements, particularly strategic bombers. Fearing an adverse reaction, Goering thought better of informing Hitler that the Soviet air force was far more powerful than he had earlier reported.

OPPOSITE: "Faster!" by Herb Block (1941):
Life races against Death as casualties at the
front grow and the birthrate of "Aryans" is
officially encouraged by the Nazi Party. By
1939, officials of the Third Reich had started
kidnapping children from other countries
whom they deemed "racially suitable for
resettlement" with German families.

ABOVE: "Oh, what will the Harvest Be?" by
Jay "Ding" Darling (1941): Hitler becomes
dimly aware of all the destruction he
has brought to Europe, but he still isn't
relinquishing his scythe.

ABOVE: "His Most Appreciative Audience" by Jay "Ding"
Darling (1941): The Three Dictators, Mussolini, Hitler and
Hirohito, put their hands together for aviator and isolationist
(if not all-out Nazi sympathizer) Charles Lindbergh, while the
American public beats a hasty retreat.

"The Boot Fits Well" by Boris Efimov (1936): Efimov was Stalin's favorite cartoonist and when Lord Beaverbrook (British Minister for Aircraft Production) went to Moscow in September 1941 he was given the above cartoon mocking the symbiotic relationship between Hitler and Mussolini as viewed by Moscow in the mid-1930s. By late 1941, Hitler's right boot (as shown here) was beginning to feel like an encumbrance.

"What Happened in Orel Echoed in Rome" by Kukryniksy (1943): This cartoon shows Hitler caught in a trap south of Orel and north of Kharkov in the biggest tank battle of all time, Kursk, in 1943. Meanwhile in Rome, Mussolini was being shown the door—ousted as leader of both the armed forces and the government by the Italian king. Not long afterward, he was rescued by German special forces in Gran Sasso.

Below: "Jack the Giant-Killer" by E. H. Shepard (1941): The Lend-Lease program, "An Act to Promote the Defense of the United States," was the banner under which the U.S. supplied Free France, Britain, China, the U.S.S.R., and other Allied nations with oil, food, and weapons from 1941 to 1945. Effectively, it marked the end of neutrality for America, which shipped over $50 billion worth of supplies.

JACK THE GIANT-KILLER

"Didn't I tell you it wasn't fair to use that sword?"

Opposite: "Time and Tide" by E. H. Shepard (1941): Hitler waits impatiently for Hermann Goering in a boat called *Pride of the Channel*. By 1941 Goering had gone from national hero to zero in Germany after the failure of the Luftwaffe to soften up Britain for invasion. Now he's going to have to swim the Channel himself, which won't be easy with all those medals on his chest. "Ready, Hermann?" Hitler says.

TIME AND TIDE

"Ready, Hermann?"

A subversive puzzle from Nazi-occupied Holland in 1942, but the kind of item that could have cost its owner his or her life if the Germans were to find it. The question, "Where is the 5th pig?," is answered by making the correct folds in the picture of the four pigs to create the image just below.

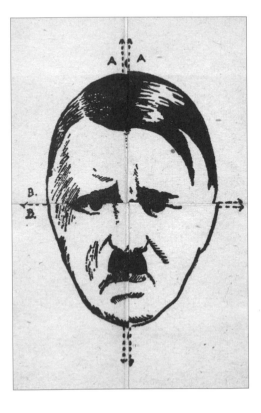

"March of the Clowns" by Albert Bloch (1941): A deliriously strange image that is full of symbols, with Hitler, who hangs from a swastika surmounted by a star, being carried at the head of a procession of clowns. In the crowd are Popeye, Olive Oyl and Krazy Kat, who are thought to represent Americans watching the conflict in Europe helplessly from afar. This picture is probably best understood as a wish-fulfilment fantasy about the defeat of Nazi Germany. Bloch was the only American-born member of the Blue Rider group founded in Munich in 1911 by Wassily Kandinsky and Franz Marc, which also included artists like Paul Klee and August Macke.

A MODERN VERSION OF THE KILKENNY CATS.

ABOVE: "A Modern Version of the Kilkenny Cats" by Clifford Berryman (1941): Kilkenny cats are Irish cats that fight to the very last. There are many versions of the story, but in Berryman's cartoon their tails are tied to the washing line, and the implication is that Hitler and Stalin will fight to the death, each consuming the other until only their tails are left.

OPPOSITE: "Just What We Wanted for Christmas Day" by Jay "Ding" Darling (1941): Hitler flees for dear life across a battlefield in which the corpses lie covered in snow as the ferocious Russian bear turns on him and sends him back where he came from.

ОДИН КОНЕЦ

Мы их побили, он их порет.
Но у него унылый вид:
Разбойник чувствует, что вскоре
Сам будет выпорот и бит.

Ц. СОЛОДАРЬ.

"This Can Only End One Way" (c.1941): Before the invasion of Russia in Operation Barbarossa, Hitler said: "I insist absolutely that my orders be executed without contradiction!" In this cartoon published in the Red Army *Pravda,* Hitler is thrashing his generals, Strauss, Halder, Guderian and Brauchitsch, for their failure to press home the three-pronged Blitzkrieg with 3 million German troops. The caption is to the effect that the Russians have beaten up the Germans and that, when they get hold of Hitler, "the villain" can expect a dose of his own medicine.

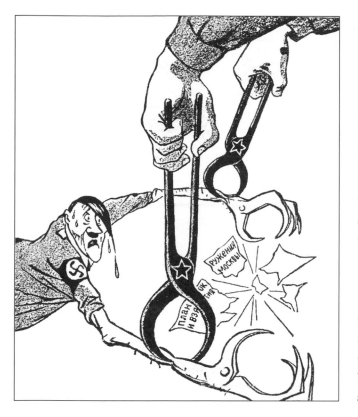

Left: "Operation Barbarossa" by Kukryniksy (1942): Hitler did not care to listen to anyone else's point of view when it came to military strategy. He could also be found as far as a thousand miles away from the front line when handing out his orders. Here, German pincer movements are outflanked by superior Soviet pincer movements, which was a very optimistic view of the situation—in fact, the Red Army was getting soundly defeated at every turn around this time.

Below: "Cannibal Vegetarian" by Kukryniksy (1941): In not so gentle fashion, Kukryniksy point out the inconsistencies in Hitler's behavior toward animals (he was vegetarian) and human beings.

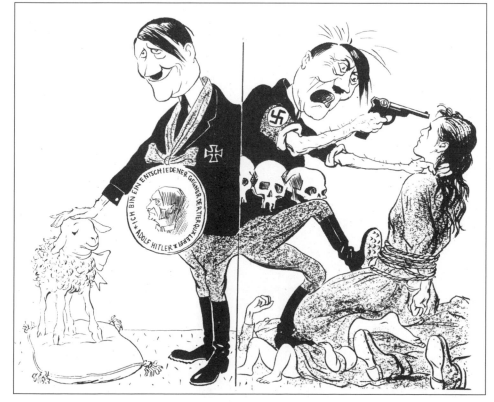

ABOVE: "I'm Sorry! It's Really Not Like This Every Day" by Clifford Berryman (1941): This commemorates the visit of Japanese Foreign Minister Yosuke Matsuoka to his Axis partners in Berlin. During the visit, there were setbacks—the Yugoslavians turned down a new Axis treaty and the Italian navy was shot up in the Mediterranean by the British. (N.B. Churchill in a sailor suit.)

LEFT: "Let the Punishment Fit the Crime" by Jay "Ding" Darling (1941): Retribution looms for the Axis leaders as the massed bombers of the Allies darken the sky.

"Hitler–Mussolini Talk" by Herb Block (1941): In the 1920s Mussolini was the top dictator in Europe, and Hitler tried to model himself on him. In September 1939, the Pact of Steel between Germany and Italy was signed, but by 1941, when a domineering Hitler met Mussolini at the Brenner Pass, Italy was seen as an unreliable ally—for instance, the Italians were unwilling to provide manpower to make up for German losses in Russia.

ABOVE: "One Prize That He Couldn't Hold" by Clifford Berryman (1941): When Hitler invaded Russia in June 1941, he was convinced he would be victorious within a year. He didn't realize the size of the task ahead. By December, he was forced to turn back from the key city of Rostov as Stalin launched his counter-offensive.

RIGHT: "There Seems To Be One Empty Chair" by Willard Combes (1941): In 1941 Rudolf Hess, then second in line to Hitler's throne after Goering, flew solo to Scotland to negotiate peace between Britain and Germany on his own initiative.

"The Catspaw" by Bernard Partridge (1941): Monkey Hitler calls on the Japanese cat to prove its loyalty by placing its paw in the fireplace of war. Japan was the third member of the Axis Alliance with Germany and Italy, and Germany was seeking to nudge its Asian friend into attacking Britain's colonies in South-East Asia, especially if that meant Singapore. In December 1941 (a few months after this cartoon appeared), Japan attacked U.S. and European territories in the Pacific, including the infamous attack on the American fleet at Pearl Harbor, Hawaii, which brought the U.S. into the war.

THE CATSPAW

" You belong to the Axis, don't you? Well, do your stuff."

"Oh, East is East and West is West, and Never the Twain Shall Meet" by Edwin Marcus (1941): The quote is from Kipling. In November 1941, German advances in North Africa were brought to a shuddering halt by British counter-attacks. It's being suggested here that this would make Hitler late to link up with Hirohito in the East under Axis plans for world domination.

UND I HAVE A DATE WITH HIROHITO

AFRICA

"Grist to the Mill on the Volga" by Boris Efimov (c.1942–3):
Hitler shovels his troops into a huge grinder operated by the
Red Army and labeled "Stalingrad," the site of what was to be a
catastrophic defeat for the German army. This probably marked
the turning point in World War II. Germany sent 3 million troops
into Russia in 1941, but it wasn't enough. However many men
Germany sent in, the Red Army had more…

THE GIANT'S ROBE

"It doesn't fit as well as I thought it would."

LEFT: "Fatty – you told me not a single bomb would fall on der Reich!" by Willard Combes (1942): Goering always found it easier to tell Hitler what he wanted to hear, rather than what was actually happening, but one day the truth was bound to catch up with him. The British and Americans had been building up their stock of bombers and, in the summer of 1942, the first thousand-bomber raids were staged over Cologne and Essen.

OPPOSITE: "The Giant's Robe" by E. H. Shepard (1942): In 1930, Hitler gave a speech in Erlangen, Bavaria in which he said that Germany, more than any other country on Earth, was predestined to rule the world. Here, the megalomaniac from Austria burrows in the dusty wardrobe of history only to discover that the ermine robe of World Domination he has coveted for so long is several sizes too big.

RIGHT: "Adolf's Easter Hat" by Jay "Ding" Darling (1942): Cartoons are a great barometer of the national mood in any country, and this U.S. effort is full of *Schadenfreude*. It doesn't look as if Adolf's new Easter bonnet will offer much protection against the conditions.

LEFT: "Petain Understands Perfectly… Now" by Jay "Ding" Darling (1942): Pierre Laval hands Marshall Petain over to Hitler like meat on the end of a piece of rope. When Allied forces, including Free French troops, defeated Axis soldiers in North Africa, and the French navy scuttled the French fleet off Toulon, the Germans decided to make their feelings known by seizing the whole of France.

"Christmas 1942" by George Fawcett (1942): New Zealand artist George Fawcett liked to produce his own Christmas cards and in 1942 he decided that Adolf Hitler would make an ideal Santa, with Ribbentrop, Goebbels and Goering as his little helpers. After a series of military blunders, Hitler seemed far less intimidating than before, and the sight of him demoted to Santa Claus could only add to the jollity of the season. The more things went wrong for him, the more his detractors rejoiced.

By permission of the Marcus family

"Home to Roost at Last!" by Edwin Marcus (1942): There was something boringly suburban about Adolf Hitler, which is subtly emphasized here by the swastika pajamas he's wearing. The plane with fangs which perches on the end of his bed is there to remind him that the wave of Allied bombings in Germany was retaliation for the Blitz when the Germans bombed the hell out of London.

ABOVE: "Ballet Russe!" by Clifford Berryman (1942): Hitler and his good friend Death note that things aren't going the way they did at Compiegne in 1940 when Germany's Blitzkrieg blew away French forces. The Russians at Stalingrad are a far tougher nut to crack, which is leading to the macabre formation dance of the German army as it heads toward the jaws of death.

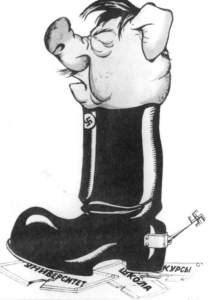

RIGHT: A small masterpiece from Russian artist Viktor Deni which shows Hitler as a destructive jackboot with the face of a pig and a swastika spur. The caption says: "University, school, education...What use has a pig for culture and science? Its horizon is extremely narrow. *Mein Kampf* is its highest achievement…" This is dated 1942.

Below: "Darkest Africa" by Edwin Marcus (1942): Dripping sweat, Hitler examines a map of Africa and is alarmed at what he sees. In the fall of 1942, the British stopped the German advance across North Africa and began a counter-attack, retaking Libya. It's almost an update of the cartoon on page 110; Marcus is making the point again in case anyone missed it the first time around.

By permission of the Marcus family

Opposite: "Der Fuehrer's Face" by Walt Disney (1942): Donald Duck throws a tomato at Hitler on the cover of the sheet music for the title song of the Walt Disney propaganda short film *Der Fuehrer's Face*, which was released in 1943. Its plot features a bad dream in which Donald Duck has a job in a factory in Nazi Germany. It won an Academy Award for Best Animated Short, the only Donald Duck film to win such an accolade, and its highlights include a band with Joseph Goebbels on trombone, Heinrich Himmler on snare drum, Hideki Tojo on sousaphone, Hermann Goering on piccolo, and Benito Mussolini on big bass drum.

AND THERE'LL BE MANY HAPPY RETURNS OF THE DAY

"And There'll Be Many Happy Returns of the Day" by Clifford Berryman (1943): April 20, 1943 was Hitler's 54th birthday and he was accustomed to getting lots of presents. Martin Bormann once gave him the Eagle's Nest on behalf of the Nazi Party; Ferdinand Porsche gave him a convertible VW, and a Munich brewery delivered special beer, since Hitler couldn't digest the ordinary stuff. The R.A.F. and the U.S. air force had special deliveries for him too!

"The Greatest Commander of All Time" by Walter Trautschold (1942–3): Hitler stands next to a gravestone marked "Stalingrad" in a setting that marks the final resting place of his ambitions. Trautschold used to appear on stage with Werner Finck, founder and star of the Berlin Catacombs club, gently satrizing the Nazis with his cartoons and illustrations for which he had briefly been imprisoned in the Esterwegen camp, Emsland in 1935.

BACK TO AN OLD ROOST.

Tuesday, February 2, 1943.

Opposite: "Back to an Old Roost" by D. R. Fitzpatrick (1943): Hitler kept singing the same old song about protecting the world from Bolshevism long after the world had tired of listening to it.

Above: "Wonder How He Stays in Business" by Jay "Ding" Darling (1943): Hitler is in charge of a department store which runs on empty promises—like his guarantee that the war would be over in a year, his assurance that enemy bombers would never reach Germany, and his promises that the German army would never retreat.

THE ROAD BACK.
WEDNESDAY, FEBRUARY 10, 1943.

Left: "The Road Back" by D. R. Fitzpatrick (1943): Hitler returns from Russia on a spectral horse, pursued by vultures and leaving behind a vast army of the dead submerged in snow. Hitler had failed to learn the lessons of Napoleon.

LEFT: "Heil!" by D. R. Fitzpatrick (1943): Death taps Hitler on the shoulder, putting in an early bid for his body and soul. It's generally thought that Hitler was responsible for the deaths of about 14 million people, including an estimated 6 million Jews during the Holocaust.

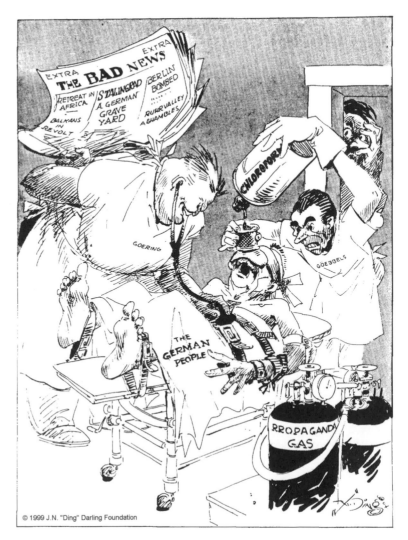

© 1999 J.N. "Ding" Darling Foundation

RIGHT: "Germany Gets the Day's News" by Jay "Ding" Darling (1943): As a stressed-looking Hitler watches from the doorway, Goering and Goebbels ensure that the German People don't get a whiff of what's really going on.

"As Inevitable as Time" by Jay "Ding" Darling (1943): Hitler asks himself where Germany's missing manpower has gone. By the end of 1944, nearly 3 million troops had perished on the Eastern Front, contrasting with the 340,000 killed on the Western Front—no wonder nobody wanted to be sent to the Eastern Front. A further 1,230,000 Germans died defending the *Vaterland* in 1945, with many more casualties elsewhere.

BUSTERS

Berryman
January 20 1943

Opposite: "Maybe You Should Have Said It Louder, Chief" by Clifford Berryman (1943): Hitler had promised the German people victory, but by January 1943 they were experiencing doubts. The Russians had broken the German blockade at Leningrad, the British retook Libya, and the Allies bombed Berlin for the first time in more than a year. "Blockbuster" was the popular name for the largest of the British bombs.

Above: "The Anti-Christ" by Arthur Szyk (1942): Polish–Jewish artist Szyk's image, with skulls reflected in the eyes and the words *Vae Victis* (Latin for "woe to the conquered") ingrained in his jet-black comb-over, shows Hitler as the personification of evil exulting in the horrors of war:

"Hitler Fighting with German Generals" by Willard Combes (1942–3): Looking like it's taken a pasting, the world lights up a cigar in relief as it watches Hitler come to blows with old-school army generals after Stalingrad and other military setbacks. Things had been going the Nazis' way for so long that it had begun to seem as if they were invincible. What a relief when they started to fight among themselves!

THE GERMANS SEEM TO BE WINNING "THE MASTER RACE."

"The Germans Seem to be Winnning 'The Master Race'" by
Clifford Berryman (1943): By 1943, the Allies had defeated the
Germans and their friends the Italians in North Africa. "The
Master Race," of course, was the term used by Hitler to imply
that the Germans, or Aryans, were destined to conquer the
world, but in this picture they don't look like they're going to.

"AWFULLY ARRAYED"

"What's the idea of the fancy costume?"

"Merely to be prepared.   I committed my chief crime in Austria: I was born there."

[The Moscow Conference has agreed that war criminals, so far as is possible, must be sent for trial to the countries where their crimes were committed.]

BELOW: "Getting Hog Tied" by Willard Combes (1944-5): In 1945, there was a black joke doing the rounds in Berlin: "Enjoy the war, peace will be much worse." By 1944, the war was already lost, but the Germans refused to surrender even though the odds against them were impossible. A self-destructive logic set in, impelling them to fight to the death and until their cities were destroyed, encouraged by Hitler who felt the German people had let him down, rather than the other way around.

OPPOSITE: "Awfully Arrayed" by Bernard Partridge (1943): Hitler sports a typically Austrian outfit of Lederhosen and Tyrolean hat, explaining to Goering he is ready in case he is returned to Austria for punishment one day. The Moscow Conference, 1943, was led by the foreign ministers of the U.S., the U.S.S.R., and the U.K. Delegates discussed ways of shortening the war as well as what should be done after the fighting was over. The title was inspired by a poem by Alaric Alexander Watts about the Siege of Belgrade (1789) conducted by the Austrian army.

ABOVE: "Hitler" by Ilia Beshkov (1944): Caricature of Hitler by the Bulgarian artist Beshkov suggesting that the ideas of the philosopher Nietzsche, including "the Superman," had helped lead to his downfall. In World War II, Bulgaria was neutral until March 1941, when it joined an alliance with the Axis powers, a situation which ended in September 1944 when the Red Army marched in. After the war, the Soviet Union installed a puppet regime.

OPPOSITE: "Festung Europa" by E. H. Shepard (1944): "Festung Europa" (Fortress Europe) was a propaganda term used by both sides during World War II. In the hands of the Germans, it meant the area of continental Europe occupied by the Nazis and held secure against the Allies. In this drawing, Hitler the Egg appears to have already had his head bashed in, but they've repainted his features at the other end, turned him around, and now he's being helped back into his eggcup to give the appearance that he's as good as new.

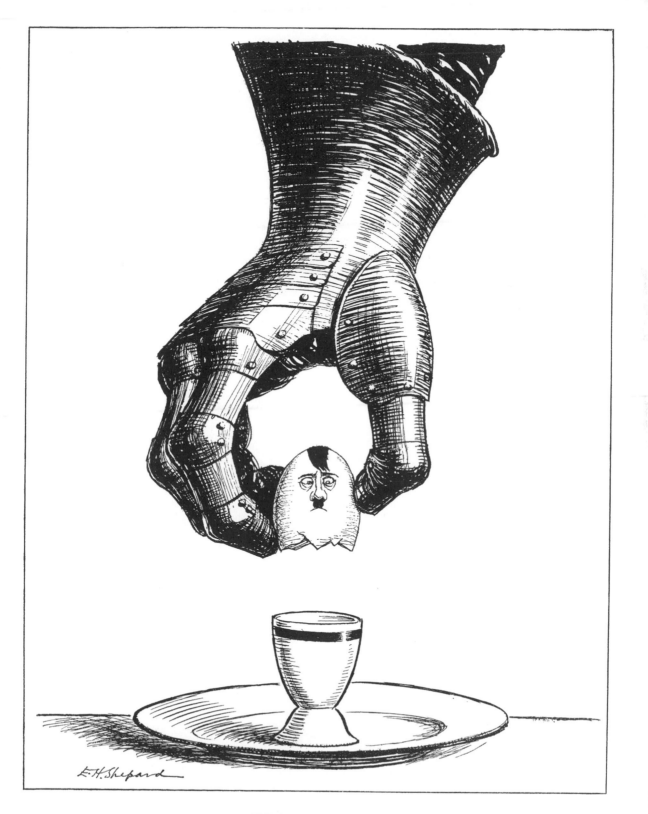

FESTUNG EUROPA

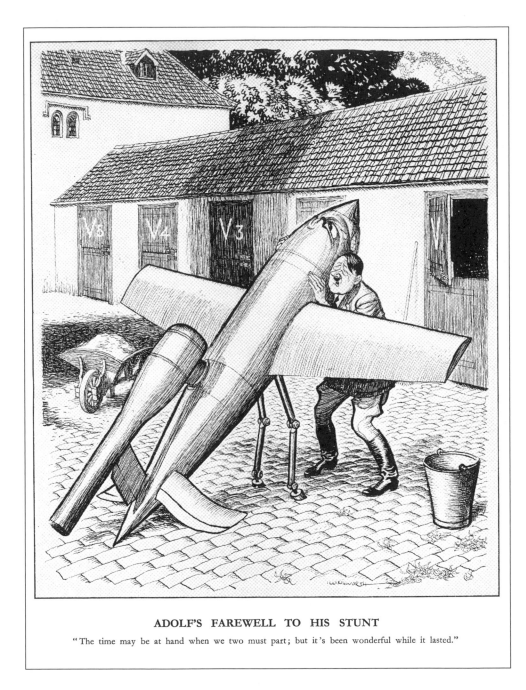

ADOLF'S FAREWELL TO HIS STUNT

"The time may be at hand when we two must part; but it's been wonderful while it lasted."

"Adolf's Farewell to his Stunt" by Illingworth (1944): Hitler told his generals that he had a secret weapon that would turn everything around. It was the V1, so called because it was a *Vergeltungswaffe*, or reprisal weapon, but also known as the "doodle bug," the "buzz-bomb," and the "cherry stone." The first one landed in Britain in June 1944, a week after D-Day, and by the end of the summer thousands of people had been killed. But aside from terrorizing the population of the south of England, they didn't really change much. They—and the V2 which followed—were just Hitler's last throw of the dice.

A "Slam the Axis" postcard from the U.S. circa 1944: Propaganda postcards like this operated at a fairly crude level. Others in the series included "Adolf's Going Places" (to Hell) and "A Royal Flush!" (Hitler, Hirohito and Mussolini are flushed down a toilet). There was so much propaganda around back then: "White" was from an acknowledged source; "Gray" mentioned no sources; "Black" pretended to be from a source other than the genuine one.

PROGRESS OF THE NEW ORDER
TUESDAY, JANUARY 25, 1944.

LEFT: "Progress of the New Order" by D. R. Fitzpatrick (1944): Hitler suffers from a hangover after his relationships with Germany's former allies have broken down. It had all seemed so intoxicating when they first fell into each other's arms…

TIGHTENING NOOSE

LEFT: "Tightening Noose" by D. R. Fitzpatrick (1944): The noose of justice seems to be heading inexorably for the neck of Adolf Hitler as a ruined town burns in the background.

"Last Chapter of 'Mein Kampf'" by D. R. Fitzpatrick (1945): The Nuremberg War Crimes Trials began in November 1945. They were perhaps the most important criminal hearings ever held because they established the principle that individuals will always be held responsible for their actions under international law. They brought closure to World War II, allowing the reconstruction of Europe to begin.

LAST CHAPTER OF "MEIN KAMPF"

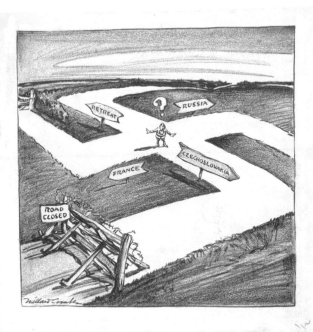

ABOVE: "Hitler at the Crossroads" by Willard Combes (1944 or 1945): A tiny figure finds his choice of destinations is becoming more and more limited. In fact there looks to be only one direction Hitler can head in, and it isn't forward.

LEFT: "Seeing Shadows" by Clifford Berryman (1944): Hitler had chosen to isolate himself from the suffering of the German people in the "Wolf's Lair," his HQ in north-eastern Germany, and in Berchtesgaden on the German–Austrian border. On July 20, 1944 senior army officers led by Claus von Stauffenberg unsuccessfully attempted to assassinate him with a bomb at the Wolf's Lair. Four ringleaders were executed by firing squad and a further eight (see left) were hanged, allegedly with piano wire for added pain. The Nazis then rounded up 5,000 people, who were executed or detained in concentration camps, as Hitler took the opportunity to purge the army and reinforce his power. This new terror also dampened the ceaseless rumblings of discontent over Hitler's role in pursuing a hopeless military struggle right to the bitter end. With this image, Berryman is suggesting there's a spare noose left over for Hitler.

БИТЫЙ ГАД

ABOVE: "Caving in on Hitler" by Willard Combes (1944–5): Anyone who has tried to put up fancy wallpaper in an irregularly shaped room will know how Hitler felt in 1944–5 as things spiraled out of control.

LEFT: "Bandaged Hitler," Russian propaganda poster (1944): The Russians had a great gift for cruelty when it came to cartoons of the enemy, and this one portrays a wounded Hitler without the tiniest grain of sympathy. Indeed, it looks like Hitler's injuries have been conjured up with large dollops of sadistic relish.

By permission of the Marcus family

"The Curfew Hour" by Edwin Marcus (1945): Slumped exhausted and sweating in a chair, Hitler looks defeated as his manpower runs out, and with it his chances of winning the war. In the West, there were more than a million Allied soldiers waiting to attack; in the East the Russian juggernaut was set to bludgeon thru Nazi defences. Soon Hitler was going to have to send in the Hitler Youth to defend Berlin. Nobody else was left!

RIGHT: A Dutch propaganda cartoon from 1945 by Smits with a title that translates as "Hail to thee in Victor's Crown," words taken from the official anthem of the German Empire (1871–1918), and formerly the royal anthem of Prussia which was sung to the stately tune of "God Save the Queen."

HEIL DIR IM SIEGESKRANZ.

OPPOSITE: "Self-Portrait of Hitler" by Mervyn Peake (c.1940s): A "connoisseur of madness in others," Peake produced a portfolio of images of war and destruction, purporting to be from the hand of the artist Adolf Hitler. In this brilliant "self-portrait," Hitler looks like a man who has gazed into the Abyss to find himself staring back.

Picture Credits

We have made every effort to contact the copyright holders of the images used in this book. In a few cases we have been unable to do so, but we will be very happy to credit them in future editions.

Tony Husband: 7

Iowa University: 11, 22, 56, 58, 59, 61 (b), 62, 95 (x2), 103, 106 (b), 114 (x2), 123 (t), 124 (b), 125

Topfoto: 8 (b), 14, 17, 48 (t), 72-3, 83, 85, 90, 96, 97, 104, 105 (b), 115, 127

State Historical Society of Missouri: 8 (t), 47, 48 (b), 65, 66 (x2), 86 (b), 122, 123 (b), 124 (t), 136 (x2), 137

Mary Evans: 9, 19, 23, 31, 32, 33, 38, 39, 42, 70, 75, 78 (t), 135, 142

Punch: 10, 27, 37, 44, 50, 51, 52, 53, 67, 74 (t), 82, 89, 92, 98, 99, 109, 112, 130, 133, 134

Getty: 12, 15, 18, 21, 24, 25, 26, 30, 35, 41, 46, 60, 61 (t), 63, 64 (t), 81, 84, 86 (t), 100, 105 (t), 111, 117 (b), 119, 121, 132, 140

Randall Bytwork: 20

Library of Congress: 28, 29, 40, 43, 54, 57, 64 (b), 68, 69, 71, 74 (b), 76-7, 79, 80, 87, 88 (b), 93, 94, 102, 106 (t), 107, 108 (x2), 110, 113, 116, 117 (t), 118, 120, 126, 128, 129, 131, 138, 139, 140 (t), 141

British Cartoon Archive, University of Kent: 34, 36, 45, 49

Mirrorpix: 78 (b), 88 (t)

Peters, Fraser and Dunlop: 143